STARS OF NASCAR

Jimmie JOHNSON

BY MATT DOEDEN

Reading Consultant:
Barbara J. Fox
Reading Specialist
North Carolina State University

Content Consultant:
Betty L. Carlan
Research Librarian
International Motorsports Hall of Fame
Talladega, Alabama

Capstone
press

Mankato, Minnesota

Blazers is published by Capstone Press,
151 Good Counsel Drive, P.O. Box 669, Mankato, Minnesota 56002.
www.capstonepress.com

Library of Congress Cataloging-in-Publication Data
Doeden, Matt.
    Jimmie Johnson / by Matt Doeden.
    p. cm. — (Blazers. Stars of NASCAR)
    Includes bibliographical references (p. 31) and index.
    Summary: "Explores the life and racing career of NASCAR Sprint Cup
champion Jimmie Johnson" — Provided by publisher.
    ISBN-13: 978-1-4296-1977-6 (hardcover)
    ISBN-10: 1-4296-1977-5 (hardcover)
    1. Johnson, Jimmie, 1975 — Juvenile literature. 2. Automobile racing drivers —
United States — Biography — Juvenile literature. I. Title. II. Series.
GV1032.J54D64 2009
796.72092 — dc22
[B]   2007052217

Essential content terms are **bold** and are defined on the spread where they first appear.

Editorial Credits
Abby Czeskleba, editor; Bobbi J. Wyss, designer; Jo Miller, photo researcher

Photo Credits
AP Images/Alamogordo Daily News, 10–11; Dave Parker, 26; Frank Polich, 14;
    John Harrell, 6–7; Russ Hamilton, 20–21; Tom Strattman, 8–9; Will Lester, 18, 19
Getty Images for NASCAR/Todd Warshaw, cover (Johnson)
Getty Images Inc./Gavin Lawrence, 22–23; Grant Halverson, 29; John Harrelson,
    cover (car); Robert Laberge, 16–17; Scott Boehm, 4–5
The Sharpe Image/Sam Sharpe, 24–25, 27
Shutterstock/Anastasios Kandris (speed and racing icons, throughout); Bocos Benedict
    (abstract digital background, throughout); Peter Kunasz, 12–13; Rzymu (flag
    background, throughout)

The publisher does not endorse products whose logos may appear on objects in
images in this book.

1 2 3 4 5 6 13 12 11 10 09 08

TABLE OF CONTENTS

KISSING THE BRICKS

Just 14 laps remained in the 2006 Allstate 400. Jimmie Johnson was in eighth place at the famous Indianapolis Motor Speedway. Jimmie had a new set of tires from a **pit stop**. He was ready to go.

pit stop — a stop that a driver makes during a race to change tires or get fuel

Jimmie's blue number 48 car was the fastest on the track. He passed car after car. With just a few laps left, he sped by Dale Earnhardt Jr. for the lead.

TRACK FACT!

Drivers race around the track 160 times at the Allstate 400.

Jimmie sailed across the finish line. He had done it! He celebrated the big win by kissing the famous strip of bricks at the Indianapolis Motor Speedway.

TRACK FACT!

Indianapolis Motor Speedway was once a brick track. Today, a narrow strip of bricks honors the track's history.

Jimmie "kissing the bricks"

9

A LOVE OF RACING

Jimmie Johnson was born September 17, 1975, in El Cajon, California. He became interested in racing at a young age. He grew up racing **dirt bikes**.

dirt bike — a lightweight motorcycle with bumps and grooves on the tires

Jimmie raced off-road trucks before
he raced stock cars. He won more than
25 off-road races. In 1998, Jimmie began
racing stock cars on the American
Speed Association (ASA) *circuit*. He
won the ASA's Rookie of the Year award.

off-road truck

circuit — a series of races that leads to a single championship

In 1998, Jimmie started driving in NASCAR's **Busch Series**. He competed in three races during his first year. In 2000, he finished 10th in the Busch Series standings.

Busch Series — NASCAR's second-highest level of competition where drivers gain experience before moving on to the Cup Series

Rick Hendrick (left), Jimmie Johnson (center),
and Jeff Gordon (right)

THE NEXT STEP

In 2000, Jimmie became
friends with NASCAR star Jeff
Gordon. Gordon asked car owner
Rick Hendrick to give Jimmie a
shot in the **Cup Series**.

Cup Series — NASCAR's highest
level of competition

Jimmie's first full Cup season was in 2002. He earned the **pole** at the season's first race, the Daytona 500. He went on to win three races in 2002.

pole — the inside spot in the front row of cars at the beginning of a race; drivers earn the pole by having the best qualifying time.

Jimmie quickly became one of the best drivers in NASCAR. He finished second in the Cup standings in both 2003 and 2004. He finished fifth in 2005.

TRACK FACT!

In 2004, Kurt Busch beat Jimmie for the championship by just eight points. It was the closest finish in NASCAR's history.

JIMMIE TODAY

The 2006 season was magical for Jimmie. He won five races, including the Daytona 500 and the Allstate 400. His great driving led him to his first Cup championship.

2006 Daytona 500

23

JIMMIE JOHNSON

24

In 2007, Jimmie and Jeff Gordon battled for the championship. Jimmie won four races in a row late in the season. He edged out Gordon and won his second straight championship.

TRACK FACT!

Jimmie beat Jeff Gordon by just 77 points for the 2007 Cup Series championship.

Jimmie is one of NASCAR's biggest stars. He is a favorite to win almost every week. He hopes one day to have as much success as his friend and teammate Jeff Gordon.

27

CUP CAREER STATISTICS

Jimmie Johnson's Cup Statistics

Year	Races	Wins	Poles	Top-5	Top-10	Winnings
2001	3	0	0	0	0	$122,320
2002	36	3	5	6	21	$2,847,702
2003	36	3	2	14	20	$5,517,850
2004	36	8	3	20	23	$5,692,624
2005	36	4	2	13	22	$6,796,664
2006	36	5	1	13	24	$8,909,143
2007	36	10	4	20	24	$7,646,421
Career	**219**	**33**	**17**	**86**	**134**	**$37,532,724**

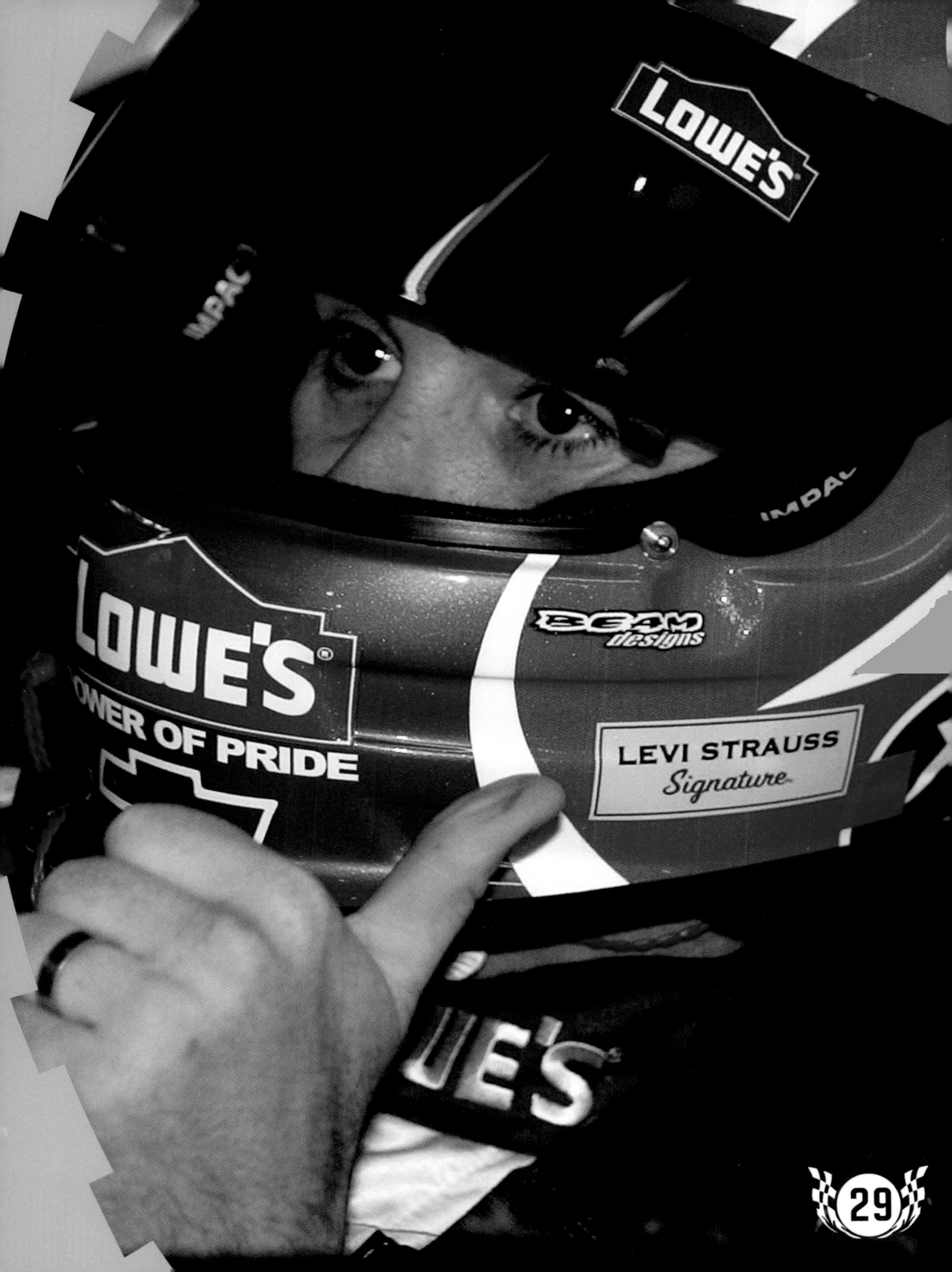
LOWE'S
LOWE'S
BEAM
designs
LEVI STRAUSS
Signature

GLOSSARY

Busch Series (BUSH SEER-eez) — NASCAR's second-highest level of competition where drivers gain experience before moving on to the Cup Series; in 2008, the series became the Nationwide Series.

circuit (SIHR-kuht) — a series of races that leads to a single championship

Cup Series — NASCAR's highest level of competition; the series has been known as the Winston Cup, the Nextel Cup, and the Sprint Cup.

dirt bike — a lightweight motorcycle used in off-road competitions

off-road — designed to be driven on dirt, mud, rock, or other rough surfaces

pit stop — a stop that a driver makes during a race to change tires or get fuel

pole — the inside spot in the front row of cars at the beginning of a race; drivers earn the pole by having the best qualifying time.

rookie (RUK-ee) — a first-year driver

success (suhk-SESS) — a good outcome or the results that were hoped for

READ MORE

Armentrout, David, and Patricia Armentrout.
Jimmie Johnson. In the Fast Lane. Vero Beach, Fla.:
Rourke, 2007.

Eagen, Rachel. *NASCAR.* Automania! New York:
Crabtree, 2007.

Farmer, Emily. *Jimmie Johnson: NASCAR Driver.*
Behind the Wheel. New York: Rosen, 2007.

INTERNET SITES

FactHound offers a safe, fun way to find Internet
sites related to this book. All of the sites
on FactHound have been
researched by our staff.

Here's how:
1. Visit *www.facthound.com*
2. Choose your grade level.
3. Type in this book ID **1429619775** for
   age-appropriate sites. You may also
   browse subjects by clicking on letters,
   or by clicking on pictures and words.
4. Click on the **Fetch It** button.

FactHound will fetch the best sites for you!

INDEX